THE
HOLY BIBLE
WHOLLY

THE HOLY BIBLE WHOLLY

**CROSSWORDS
WORDFINDS
QUIZZES
AND MORE
FROM THE OLD AND NEW
TESTAMENTS**

HAZEL JAYCOX BROWN

Abingdon Press / Nashville

THE HOLY BIBLE WHOLLY

Copyright © 1994 by Abingdon Press

94 95 96 97 98 99 00 01 02 03—10 9 8 7 6 5 4 3 2 1

This book is printed on acid-free, recycled paper.

ISBN 0-687-38333-1

MANUFACTURED IN THE UNITED STATES OF AMERICA

To David,
my dear husband
my pastor
my teacher
my encourager in personal ministry
for nearly four decades now,
and
most recently
my at-home editor
and technical advisor

Acknowledgment

I am grateful to my prayer partners, those women in our weekly Bible study and precious friends from here (Seiling, Oklahoma) who have prayed faithfully for me in this project. They will never understand how much those prayers made a difference.

Preface

Have you ever noticed that *SWORD* is *WORD* with an *S* in front of it? In Ephesians 6 the sword is mentioned as part of the full armor of God that we are to put on (vv. 11, 13). Verse 17 says that the Sword of the Spirit is the Word of God."

Swords get dull at times, and to be effective they must be sharpened. These Bible puzzles and quizzes are a way to sharpen your Sword and your mind.

Scriptures in this book are taken from the New International Version unless otherwise noted. Helpful references are included in most activities, so feel free to use your Bible. Many of these puzzles and quizzes are in reality mini-Bible studies. They will teach, refresh your memories, and serve as good mind-reinforcers. You will sharpen your mind and learn more about God from His Word. Wonderful growth will take place.

Read the Scripture at the beginning again. That is a promise. We will be ever bearing fresh fruit as we study and live by God's Word. God isn't finished with us yet. He has wonderful plans as we follow Him.

Gentlemen, women, are you ready?

BEGIN! SHARPEN YOUR SWORDS!

Contents

NEW SEARCH FOR OLD TESTAMENT BOOKS

Books in the puzzle below are printed vertically, horizontally, or diagonally; some are backward. Books like 1 Samuel and 2 Samuel are combined into one—Samuel, Kings, and Chronicles. One book is missing. Circle each of the thirty-five names that appears in the puzzle. Use the table of contents of your Bible to help you.

```
Z  L  E  I  N  A  D  I  H  C  A  L  A  M
Y  E  J  H  A  I  N  A  H  P  E  Z  H  S
M  I  U  O  E  P  G  S  H  I  A  S  A  H
O  K  D  S  E  C  E  N  A  H  U  M  N  J
N  E  G  E  S  L  N  O  H  C  U  R  O  I
O  Z  E  A  T  O  E  I  I  E  N  B  J  S
R  E  S  I  H  C  S  T  L  H  O  S  L  A
E  C  C  L  E  S  I  A  S  T  E  S  E  I
T  H  P  S  R  V  S  T  J  O  S  H  U  A
U  A  R  Z  E  O  J  N  I  A  G  G  A  H
E  R  O  L  N  E  H  E  M  I  A  H  F  A
D  I  V  B  H  A  I  M  E  R  E  J  O  C
M  A  E  I  H  A  B  A  K  K  U  K  G  I
C  H  R  O  N  I  C  L  E  S  L  N  R  M
H  O  B  A  D  I  A  H  E  X  O  D  U  S
A  N  S  R  E  B  M  U  N  S  O  M  T  O
P  S  A  L  M  S  G  N  I  K  R  U  H  T
```

THE BOOK MISSING FROM THE PUZZLE IS_____

ANSWERS for "New Search for Old Testament Books":

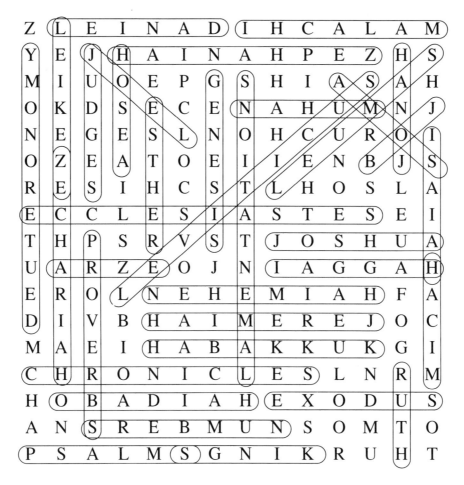

THE BOOK MISSING FROM THE PUZZLE IS ___ Song of Songs (Solomon)

I ORDER YOU

List the books of the Bible in order. A clue at the end of each line tells the number of letters in each name. Another help names every fourth book for you. If you list them all without looking in your Bible, that is impressive. If you list them without a spelling error, that is doubly impressive.

OLD TESTAMENT

I. PENTATEUCH (Books of Law)

1. _____(7)
2. _____(6)
3. _____(9)
4. ____Numbers_____(7)
5. _____(11)

III. POETRY

1. _____(3)
2. _____(6)
3. ____Proverbs_____(8)
4. _____(12)
5. _____(3 words)

IV. MAJOR PROPHETS

1. _____(6)
2. ____Jeremiah_____(8)
3. _____(12)
4. _____(7)
5. _____(6)

II. HISTORY (After Moses)

1. _____(6)
2. _____(6)
3. ____Ruth_____(4)
4. 1 _____(6)
5. 2 _____(6)
6. 1 _____(5)
7. 2 ___Kings_____(5)
8. 1 _____(10)
9. 2 _____(10)
10. _____(4)
11. ___Nehemiah_____(8)
12. _____(6)

V. MINOR PROPHETS

1. ____Hosea_____(5)
2. _____(4)
3. _____(4)
4. _____(7)
5. ____Jonah_____(5)

6. _____(5)
7. _____(5)
8. _____(8)

9.   Zephaniah
_____(9)
10. _____(6)
11. _____(9)
12. _____(7)

NEW TESTAMENT

I. GOSPELS

1.   Matthew _____(7)
2. _____(4)
3. _____(4)
4. _____(4)

IV. OTHER EPISTLES (Letters)

1. _____(7)
2. _____(5)
3. 1 _____(5)
4. 2 _____(5)
5. 1 _____(4)
6. 2   John _____(4)
7. 3 _____(4)
8. _____(4)

II. HISTORY (After Resurrection)

1.   Acts _____(4)

III. PAUL'S EPISTLES (Letters)

1. _____(6)
2. 1 _____(11)
3. 1 _____(11)
4.   Galatians _____(9)
5. _____(9)
6. _____(11)
7. _____(10)
8. 1 Thessalonians _____(13)
9. 2 _____(13)
10. 1 _____(7)
11. 2 _____(7)
12.   Titus _____(5)
13. _____(8)

V. PROPHECY

1. _____(10)

....

OLD TESTAMENT

   I. PENTATEUCH—Genesis, Exodus, Leviticus, Numbers, Deuteronomy.
  II. HISTORY—Joshua, Judges, Ruth, 1 Samuel, 2 Samuel, 1 Kings, 2 Kings, 1 Chronicles, 2 Chronicles, Ezra, Nehemiah, Esther.
 III. POETRY—Job, Psalms, Proverbs, Ecclesiastes, Song of Songs (Solomon).
 IV. MAJOR PROPHETS—Isaiah, Jeremiah, Lamentations, Ezekiel, Daniel
  V. MINOR PROPHETS—Hosea, Joel, Amos, Obadiah, Jonah, Micah, Nahum, Habakkuk, Zephaniah, Haggai, Zechariah, Malachi.

NEW TESTAMENT

   I. GOSPELS—Matthew, Mark, Luke, John.
  II. HISTORY—Acts
 III. PAUL'S EPISTLES—Romans, 1 Corinthians, 2 Corinthians, Galatians, Ephesians, Philippians, Colossians, 1 Thessalonians, 2 Thessalonians, 1 Timothy, 2 Timothy, Titus, Philemon
 IV. OTHER EPISTLES—Hebrews, James, 1 Peter, 2 Peter, 1 John, 2 John, 3 John, Jude.
  V. PROPHECY—Revelation.

TURN OVER FOR ANSWERS TO "I ORDER YOU."

....

RUNNING THE RACE

This race against time has a twofold purpose: (1) to read verses about how to live your Christian life and (2) to improve your ability to find Scripture references quickly (an old-fashioned Sword drill).

Procedure: 1. Find the verse. 2. Read it through. 3. Then count to whatever word number is noted after the verse. Write that word on the appropriate line in the shoe. When finished, read the verse in the shoe.

Completing this exercise in 20 minutes is reasonable. If in 15 minutes, that is very good. If you do it in less than 12, then you're faster than I am. Congratulations!

1. Prov. 4:12—word 13

2. Acts 3:1—word 6

3. Gal. 2:2—word 37

4. Prov. 18:10—word 7

5. Nah. 1:15—word 12

6. Heb. 12:1—word 34

7. Isa. 40:31—word 3

8. Dan. 9:26—word 10

9. 2 John 9—word 20

10. Ps. 40:2—word 19

11. Rom. 16:20—word 20

12. 2 Kings 4:29—word 17

13. 2 Tim. 4:7—word 14

14. 1 Cor. 9:24—word 2

15. Isa. 10:3—word 13

16. Deut. 8:20—word 16

17. Eccles. 9:11—word 27

18. 1 Pet. 1:22—word 10

STARTING TIME (on the clock): _____

FINISHING TIME: _____

TIME TAKEN: _____ minutes.

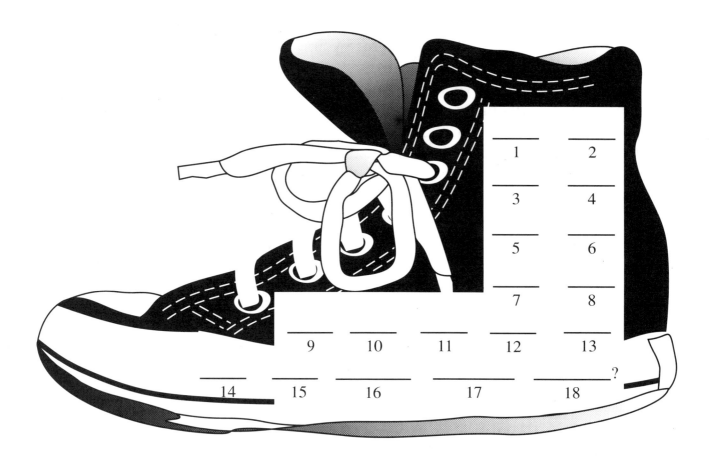

TURN OVER FOR ANSWERS TO "RUNNING THE RACE."

"You were running a good race. Who cut in on you and kept you from obeying the truth?"
Gal. 5:7

WE'LL CROSS THAT WORD WHEN WE GET THERE

and

ACROSS

1. Abraham's first home: _____ of Chaldeans. Neh. 9:7
4. Spent time in the belly of a sea animal. Matt. 12:40
5. Doctor, writer, companion of Paul. Col. 4:14
6. Son of Jacob. Gen. 30:6
7. A bald-headed prophet of God. 2 Kings 2:23
12. The Book of Beginnings in the Bible.
13. Brother of Rebekah. Gen. 24:29
14. A very tall Philistine soldier. 1 Sam. 17:4
16. First hunter mentioned in the Bible. Gen. 10:9
19. Abigail's not-very-nice husband. 1 Sam. 25:3
20. Moses' mother. Exod. 6:20.

DOWN

1. Where Job lived. Job 1:1
2. First lied, then died; husband, then wife. Acts 5:1-9
3. Evil king of Israel married to Jezebel. 1 Kings 16:30, 31
4. An Old Testament reckless driver. 2 Kings 9:20
5. Jacob's first wife. Gen. 29:21-25
8. Cloth around Jesus' dead body. Matt. 27:59
9. A handsome son of a king. 2 Sam. 14:25, 26
10. Heber's wife who killed Sisera. Judg. 4:17
11. _____, King of Bashan owned a very long bed. Deut. 3:11
15. Prophetess who knew baby Jesus was Messiah. Luke 2:36.
17. Father of Micaiah the prophet. 1 Kings 22:8
18. Played a harp for the king. 1 Sam. 16:23

TURN OVER FOR ANSWERS TO
"WE'LL CROSS THAT WORD WHEN WE GET THERE"

DOWN

1. Uz
2. Ananias, Sapphira
3. Ahab
4. Jehu
5. Leah
8. linen
9. Absalom
10. Jael
11. Og
15. Anna
17. Imlah
18. David

ACROSS

1. Ur
4. Jonah
5. Luke
6. Dan
7. Elisha
12. Genesis
13. Laban
14. Goliath
16. Nimrod
19. Nabal
20. Jochebed

ARE YOU SURE?

Below are familiar quotations. Some are from the Bible and some aren't. Write *true* on the lines you believe are accurate quotations from the King James Version of the Bible.

_____ 1. "The fear of the Lord is the beginning of wisdom."

_____ 2. "Cleanliness is next to godliness."

_____ 3. "Wealth maketh many friends, but the poor is separated from his neighbour."

_____ 4. "But he that keepeth the law, happy is he."

_____ 5. "For money is the root of all evil."

_____ 6. "For what shall it profit a man, if he shall gain the whole world, and lose his own soul?"

_____ 7. "The race is not to the swift, nor the battle to the strong."

_____ 8. "And if a house be divided against itself, that house cannot stand."

_____ 9. "It was said of the disciples, 'Behold, how they loved one another.' "

_____ 10. "Blessed is he who has found his work; let him ask no other blessedness."

_____ 11. "If God be for us, who can be against us?"

_____ 12. "But he that hateth his brother is in darkness, and walketh in the darkness, and knoweth not whither he goeth, because that darkness hath blinded his eyes."

_____ 13. "Pride and grace dwelt never in one place."

_____ 14. "If thou thinkest twice before thou speakest once, thou wilt speak twice the better for it."

_____ 15. "Pride goeth before destruction, and an haughty spirit before a fall."

_____ 16. "Pure religion and undefiled before God and the Father is this, To visit the fatherless and widows in their affliction, and to keep himself unspotted from the world."

_____ 17. "The quality of mercy is not strained; It droppeth as the gentle rain from heaven Upon the place beneath. It is twice blessed—It blesseth him that gives, and him that takes."

_____ 18. "Greater love hath no man than this, that a man lay down his life for his friends."

_____ 19. "He breaks the power of canceled sin, He sets the prisoner free, His blood can make the foulest clean—His blood availed for me."

_____ 20. "God is not dead, nor doth He sleep; The wrong shall fail, the right prevail, With peace on earth, good-will to men."

_____ 21. "A merry heart doeth good like a medicine."

_____ 22. "A good name is rather to be chosen than great riches, and loving favour rather than silver and gold."

_____ 23. "I know that, whatsoever God doeth, it shall be for ever."

_____ 24. "Follow peace with all men, and holiness, without which no man shall see the Lord."

_____ 25. "Misery acquaints a man with strange bedfellows."

HELPFUL SCRIPTURE REFERENCES: Ps. 111:10. Prov. 9:10; 16:18; 17:22; 19:4; 22:1, 29:18. Eccles. 3:14; 9:11. Mark 3:25; 8:36. John 13:35; 15:13. Rom. 8:31. 1 Tim. 6:10. Heb. 12:14. James 1:27. 1 John 2:11.

TURN OVER FOR
ANSWERS TO "ARE YOU SURE?":
(Bible quotations—King James Version)

1. True—Ps. 111:10; Prov. 9:10. 2. False—John Wesley. 3. True. 4. True—Prov. 19:4. 5. False—"The love of money is the root . . ."—1 Tim. 6:10. 6. True—Mark 29:18. 7. True—Eccles. 9:11. 8. True—Mark 3:25. 9. False—probably a misquotation from John 13:35. 10. False—Thomas Carlyle. 11. True—Rom. 8:31. 12. True—1 John 2:11. 13. False—James Kelly. 14. False—William Penn. 15. True—Prov. 16:18. 16. True—James 1:27. 17. False—William Shakespeare. 18. True—John 15:13. 19. False—Charles Wesley's "O for a Thousand Tongues." 20. False—Henry W. Longfellow's "I Heard the Bells on Christmas Day." 21. True—Prov. 17:22. 22. True—Prov. 22:1. 23. True—Eccles. 3:14. True—Heb. 12:14. 25. False—William Shakespeare.

NAME DROPPING

Mark out the name that doesn't belong. Then tell what group the remaining three are. Example: Crimson, black, ~~bleat~~, purple. Group—*colors*. Scripture helps are listed below.

GROUP

1. Hezekiah, Jonah, Job, Ezra _____
2. John the Baptist, Mary, Elizabeth, Luke _____
3. 1 Kings, Hebrews, Haggai, Nahum _____
4. Jeroboam, Joshua, Saul, Asa _____
5. Elijah, Ezekiel, Isaac, Isaiah _____
6. Joanna, Dorcas, Priscilla, Rebekah _____
7. Rahab, Ruth, Reah, Rachel _____
8. Judges, Genesis, Numbers, Leviticus _____
9. Luke, Matthew, 1 John, Mark _____
10. Titus, Philemon, 1 Peter, 2 Timothy _____
11. Samuel, Samson, Miriam, Deborah _____
12. Ahab, Job, Moses, Daniel _____
13. Peter, Philip, John, Joseph _____
14. Dan, Jehu, Reuben, Simeon _____
15. Methuselah, Abel, Adam, Enoch _____

SCRIPTURE HELPS

1. Look at the books of the Bible or the second activity in this book.
2. Luke 1:5, 13, 34-36.
3. See books of the Bible or second activity in this book.
4. 1 Chron. 3:10; 5:10, 17; 7:27.
5. Gen. 25:5; 1 Kings 18:36; Isa. 37:2; Ezek. 12:17-28.
6. Gen. 24:67; Luke 8:3; Acts 9:36; 18:2.

7. Gen. 30:1; Josh. 2:1; 6:17; Ruth 2:2.
8. See books of the Bible or second activity.
9. See books of the Bible or second activity.
10. See books of the Bible or second activity.
11. Exod. 15:20, 21; Judg. 4:4, 5; 15:20; 1 Sam. 7:15, 17.
12. Deut. 34:5; 1 Kings 21:25-26; Job 1:1; Dan. 9.
13. Matt. 10:2-4.
14. Num. 1.
15. Gen. 4, 5.

TURN OVER FOR ANSWERS TO
"NAME DROPPING"

15. Abel/Lived to be old
14. Jehu/Tribes of Israel or sons of Jacob
13. Joseph/Twelve Apostles
12. Ahab/Godly men
11. Miriam/Judges
10. 1 Peter/Paul's letters or Pastoral Epistles
9. 1 John/Gospels
8. Judges/Books of Moses or Law or Pentateuch
7. Reah/Old Testament women or women of the Bible
6. Rachel/New Testament women
5. Isaac/Prophets
4. Joshua/Kings
3. Hebrews/Books of the Old Testament
2. Luke/Relatives of Jesus
1. Hezekiah/Books of the Bible or Old Testament

Mark out/The remaining group are:

ANGEL APPEARANCES

Choose one answer for each question below. You may use helpful Scriptures given at the end of the quiz.

_____ 1. Gabriel appeared to this young maiden telling her she would become mother of the Son of God. She was: (a) Mara, (b) Michal, (c) Miriam, (d) Mary.

_____ 2. An angel appeared on two occasions to the mother of Ishmael. She was: (a) Hannah, (b) Huldah, (c) Hagar, (d) Hadassah.

_____ 3. Two angels rescued this man and his family from Sodom. He was: (a) Isaac, (b) Job, (c) Ira, (d) Lot.

_____ 4. On a ship headed for Rome, they were about to be shipwrecked when an angel of God appeared and reassured this man of everyone's safety. He was: (a) Paul, (b) Peter, (c) Philip, (d) Phinehas.

_____ 5. The angel of the Lord stood in the way of a donkey and his master. The master was: (a) Balaam, (b) Boaz, (c) Barabbas, (d) Bartholomew.

_____ 6. An angel of the Lord appeared to this man in a burning bush. He was: (a) Abraham, (b) Gideon, (c) Moses, (d) Joshua.

_____ 7. This imprisoned man was sleeping when the angel came, released his chains and led him out of jail. He was: (a) Silas, (b) Peter, (c) John the Baptist, (d) James.

_____ 8. Depressed because Jezebel vowed to kill this prophet, he went to the wilderness where an angel prepared food for him. He was: (a) Elijah, (b) Enoch, (c) Eli, (d) Elihu.

_____ 9. An angel told this barren woman she'd finally have a son. Later, the angel reappeared repeating his command that this young man was to be a Nazarite. The son was: (a) Samuel, (b) Salmon, (c) Samson, (d) Solomon.

_____ 10. In answer to his prayers, an angel told this Gentile to send for Peter at Joppa. The Gentile was: (a) Luke, (b) Titus, (c) Cornelius, d. Barnabas.

....

_____ 11. An angel of the Lord told this man to go to Gaza. There an Ethiopian eunuch was converted. The man was: (a) Paul, (b) Philip, (c) Peter, (d) Philemon.

_____ 12. Gabriel appeared to this Old Testament prophet twice—to explain things he failed to understand. (a) Jonah, (b) Elijah, (c) Daniel, (d) Hosea.

HELPFUL SCRIPTURES: (1) Luke 1:26-38; (2) Gen. 16:1-12; (3) Gen. 19:1-22; (4) Acts 27:21-25; (5) Num. 22:22-35; (6) Exod. 3–4:17; (7) Acts 12:1-19; (8) 1 Kings 19:1-8; (9) Judg. 13:1-20; (10) Acts 10:1-8; (11) Acts 8:26-39; (12) Dan. 8:16, 9:21.

TURN OVER FOR ANSWERS TO
"ANGEL APPEARANCES."

1. d, 2. c, 3. d, 4. a, 5. a, 6. c, 7. b, 8. a, 9. c, 10. c, 11. b, 12. c

....

HOW LONG, O LORD?

Below are clues with a reference that will provide you a number between 1 and 25. None will appear more than once. In order to keep track of the numbers you have used, once you determine the number, place the letter of the clue in the box of the same number.

1	2	3	4	5
6	7	8	9	10
11	12	13	14	15
16	17	18	19	20
21	22	23	24	25

CLUES AND LOCATION

A. Jereboam reigned __?__ years over Israel. 1 Kings 14:20
B. "No man can serve __?__ masters." Matt. 6:24
C. Josiah was __?__ years old when he became king. 2 Kings 22:1
D. Jehoshaphat reigned in Jerusalem for __?__ years. 2 Chron. 20:31
E. Age of Uzziah when he became king. 2 Chron. 26:1
F. In the __?__th year of Nebuchadnezzar's reign, his commander set fire to the temple and most of Jerusalem. Jer. 52:12, 13
G. __?__ leper came back to Jesus to thank him for healing. Luke 17:15-17

H. The ark of the covenant was at Kiriath Jearim for __?__ years. 1 Sam. 7:2

I. Zedekiah was __?__ years old when he began to reign. 2 Kings 24:18

J. Total number of fingers and toes on this huge man. 2 Sam. 21:20

K. The number of years the woman had been afflicted whom Jesus healed. Luke 13:11

L. Jonah spent __?__ days in the belly of a huge fish. Matt. 12:40

M. Jesus appeared to __?__ disciples at mealtime in Jerusalem the evening after the resurrection. Mark 16:14

N. __?__ apostles of the Lamb. Rev. 21:14

O. Hosea bought his wife back for __?__ shekels of silver and some barley. Hos. 3:1, 2

P. The king of Canaan had __?__ hundred chariots of iron. Judg. 4:3

Q. The word tithe means one __?__th . (Dictionary)

R. The Samaritan woman had had __?__ husbands. John 4:18

S. Tola led Israel as a judge for __?__ years. Judg. 10:1, 2

T. From Abraham to David were __?__ generations Matt. 1:17

U. God created everything in __?__ days. Gen. 1

V. __?__ men, full of the Spirit and wisdom, were chosen to relieve the apostles of some of their work. Acts 6:3

W. Jacob lived __?__ years in the land of Egypt. Gen. 47:28

X. Lazarus was dead __?__ days before Jesus came. John 11:17

Y. It took Solomon __?__ years to complete the building of his palace. 1 Kings 7:1

TURN OVER FOR ANSWERS TO
"HOW LONG, O LORD?"

1 G	2 B	3 L	4 X	5 R
6 U	7 V	8 C	9 P	10 Q
11 M	12 N	13 Y	14 T	15 O
16 E	17 W	18 K	19 F	20 H
21 I	22 A	23 S	24 J	25 D

READING THE GREEK WAY

The New Testament was written in Greek without punctuation or spaces between words. They used vowels, but finding where words began and ended was sometimes hard. That can be difficult even in English. Try reading these verses:

IAMTHEGOODSHEPHERDIKNOWMYSHEEPANDMYSHEEPKNOWME

JUSTASTHEFATHERKNOWSMEANDIKNOWTHEFATHERANDILAY

DOWNMYLIFEFORTHESHEEP

A slash mark between words helps. Find thirty-four words. Write down the words as you recognize them:

_____

_____

_____

_____

John 10:14, 15

Try another a bit more difficult (38 words):

THEREFORESINCEWEARESURROUNDEDBYSUCHAGREATCLO

UDOFWITNESSESLETUSTHROWOFFEVERYTHINGTHATHINDERSA

NDTHESINTHATSOEASILYENTANGLESANDLETUSRUNWITHPERS

EVERANCETHERACEMARKEDOUTFORUS

_____

_____

....

_____

_____

_____

Heb. 12:1

Now for a real challenge, try this from the King James Version (81 words):

FORITESTIFYUNTOEVERYMANTHATHEARETHTHEWORDSOFTHEP
ROPHECYOFTHISBOOKIFANYMANSHALLADDUNTOTHESETHINGS
GODSHALLADDUNTOHIMTHEPLAGUESTHATAREWRITTENINTHIS
BOOKANDIFANYMANSHALLTAKEAWAYFROMTHEWORDSOFTHE
BOOKOFTHISPROPHECYGODSHALLTAKEAWAYHISPA
RTOUTOFTHEBOOKOFLIFEANDOUTOFTHEHOLYCITYANDFROM
THETHINGSWHICHAREWRITTENINTHISBOOK

Write it here:

_____

_____

_____

_____

_____

_____

Now compare with Rev. 22:18, 19 KJV.

....

As you read the Bible, thank God for the hard work of translators. Isn't it wonderful to read God's precious Word?

TURN OVER FOR ANSWERS TO
"READING THE GREEK WAY."

John 10:14, 15—'' ' I am the good shepherd; I know my sheep and my sheep know me—just as the Father knows me and I know the Father—and I lay down my life for the sheep.' ''

Heb. 12:1—''Therefore, since we are surrounded by such a great cloud of witnesses, let us throw off everything that hinders and the sin that so easily entangles, and let us run with perseverance the race marked out for us.''

Rev. 22:18, 19 KJV—''For I testify unto every man that heareth the words of the prophecy of this book, If any man shall add unto these things, God shall add unto him the plagues that are written in this book: And if any man shall take away from the words of the book of this prophecy, God shall take away his part out of the book of life, and out of the holy city, and from the things which are written in this book.''

READING THE HEBREW WAY

Most of the Old Testament was written in Hebrew. Reading it was more difficult than Greek because no vowels appeared in their words. Neither did they leave spaces between words nor use any of our punctuation markings. To get an idea of a translator's job, here is such a verse in English. This familiar Old Testament verse has nine words: (Slash marks placed between words are helpful.)

THLRDSMSHPHRDSHLLNTWNT

_____

_____

See how helpful spaces between words, vowels, and punctuation are? That verse is Ps. 23:1 (KJV).

Try another familiar Old Testament verse. These 22 words are from the NIV:

SGDCRTDMNNHSWNMGNTHMGFGDHCRTDHMMLNDFMLHCRTDTHM

_____

_____

_____

Gen. 1:27 NIV.

Now try this brain buster of 31 words:

HWBTFLNTHMNTNSRTHFTFTHSWHBRNGGDNWSWHPRCLMPC
WHBRNGGDTDNGSWHPRCLMSLVTNWHSTZNYRGDRGNS

_____

_____

_____

_____

Compare what you have to Isa. 52:7 NIV.

TURN OVER FOR ANSWERS TO
"READING THE HEBREW WAY."

Ps. 23:1—"'The Lord is my shepherd; I shall not want.'" (KJV)

Gen. 1:27—"'So God created man in his own image, in the image of God he created him; male and female he created them.'"

Isa. 52:7—"'How beautiful on the mountains are the feet of those who bring good news, who proclaim peace, who bring good tidings, who proclaim salvation, who say to Zion, 'Your God reigns!'"

WHO'S NEXT?

Two sets are listed below. The first is Old Testament men and the second, Old Testament events. Each group is out of order time-wise, i.e., when a person lived or when an event happened. Number them chronologically: 1 to 10. Helpful Scriptures are found below the lists.

I. MEN OF THE OLD TESTAMENT

_____ Moses

_____ Noah

_____ Ezra

_____ Isaiah

_____ David

_____ Abraham

_____ Adam

_____ Joseph

_____ Gideon

_____ Elijah

HELPFUL SCRIPTURES: 1 Chron. 1:1, 3, 28; 1 Chron. 2:1, 2; Exod. 2; Judg. 6; 1 Sam. 16; 1 Kings 17; 2 Kings 19:2; Neh. 8:1

II. OLD TESTAMENT EVENTS

_____ The victory over Jericho

_____ The Exodus from Egypt

_____ The Tower of Babel

_____ The captivity of the northern kingdom (Israel)

_____ The giving of the Law

....

_____ The completion of Solomon's temple
_____ The captivity of the southern kingdom (Judah)
_____ The Flood
_____ Rebuilding the temple completed under Zerubbabel
_____ Israel given first king

HELPFUL SCRIPTURES: Gen. 6–8; Gen. 11:1-9; Exod. 12-14; Exod. 20:1-17; Josh. 6; 1 Sam. 9-12; 1 Kings 6:38; 2 Kings 17; 2 Kings 24, 25; Ezra 5, 6

TURN OVER FOR ANSWERS FOR "WHO'S NEXT?"

6 Israel given first king
10 Rebuilding the temple completed under Zerubbabel
1 The Flood
9 The captivity . . . southern kingdom (Judah)
7 The completion of Solomon's temple
4 The giving of the Law
8 The captivity . . . northern kingdom (Israel)
2 The Tower of Babel
3 The Exodus from Egypt
5 The victory over Jericho

II. OLD TESTAMENT EVENTS

8 Elijah
6 Gideon
4 Joseph
1 Adam
3 Abraham
7 David
9 Isaiah
10 Ezra
2 Noah
5 Moses

I. MEN OF THE OLD TESTAMENT

....

38

THEN WHAT HAPPENED?

Two sets are listed below. The first is events in the life of Christ, and the second, events in the book of Acts. Each list has ten, but are out of chronological order. Number each group in order—1 for the earliest. Helpful Scriptures are below each list.

I. EVENTS IN THE LIFE OF CHRIST

_____ The crucifixion

_____ Jesus' Discourse in the Upper Room

_____ The temptation

_____ The resurrection

_____ Jesus' first public miracle at wedding at Cana

_____ Nicodemus meets Jesus at night

_____ Christ's agonizing time in Gethsemane

_____ The triumphal entry into Jerusalem

_____ The raising of Lazarus from the dead

_____ Jesus' trial before Pilate

HELPFUL SCRIPTURES: Matthew 4:1-11; John 2, 3, 11, 12, 13-17, 18, 19, 20.

II. EVENTS IN THE BOOK OF ACTS

_____ Paul and Barnabas go on missionary journey

_____ Healing of lame man by Peter and John

_____ The Jerusalem Council

_____ Paul shipwrecked on the way to Rome

_____ Pentecost, and the Holy Spirit given

_____ Stephen martyred

_____ The Gospel and Holy Spirit given to Gentiles too

_____ Disciples first called Christians
_____ Saul converted
_____ Paul spends three years at Ephesus

HELPFUL SCRIPTURES: Acts 2:1-12; 3:1-11; 7; 9:1-20; 10:44-45; 11:26; 13:2, 3; 15:1-35; 20:17-31; 27.

TURN OVER FOR ANSWERS TO
"THEN WHAT HAPPENED?"

9 Paul spends three years at Ephesus
4 Saul converted
6 Disciples first called Christians
5 The Gospel and Holy Spirit given to Gentiles too
3 Stephen martyred
1 Pentecost, and the Holy Spirit given
10 Paul shipwrecked on the way to Rome
8 The Jerusalem Council
2 Healing of lame man by Peter and John
7 Paul and Barnabas go on missionary journey

II. EVENTS IN THE BOOK OF ACTS

8 Jesus' trial before Pilate
4 The raising of Lazarus from the dead
5 The triumphal entry into Jerusalem
7 Christ's agonizing time in Gethsemane
3 Nicodemus meets Jesus at night
2 Jesus' first public miracle at wedding at Cana
10 The resurrection
1 The temptation
6 Jesus' Discourse in the Upper Room
9 The crucifixion

I. EVENTS IN THE LIFE OF CHRIST

I FOUND IT! I FOUND IT!

If someone asked you where a familiar Bible passage was located, could you answer? Do you know your Old Testament well enough to quickly locate well-known events or special scriptures? Try matching these. Use your Bible, if necessary, then memorize their location.

_____ 1. The Creation Story

_____ 2. Noah and the Flood

_____ 3. Daniel in the Lion's Den

_____ 4. Famous Chapter on Tithing

_____ 5. The Ten Commandments (2)

_____

_____ 6. The Shepherd's Psalm

_____ 7. Baby Moses Found in the Nile

_____ 8. The Passover's Origin

_____ 9. Three Men in a Fiery Furnace

_____ 10. The Shortest Psalm

_____ 11. The Longest Psalm

_____ 12. David and Goliath

_____ 13. Joshua and Battle at Jericho

_____ 14. Prophecy of the Suffering Messiah

_____ 15. Thanksgiving Psalm

_____ 16. The Valley of Dry Bones

_____ 17. Abraham

_____ 18. The sun stands still

_____ 19. Building the First Temple

_____ 20. Rebuilding the Temple

a. Malachi 3

b. Psalm 119

c. Genesis 12–25

d. Exodus 12

e. Genesis 1, 2

f. Isaiah 53

g. Genesis 6–9

h. Psalm 117

i. Psalm 100

j. 1 Samuel 17

k. Exodus 2

l. Exodus 20

m. Ezekiel 37

n. Deuteronomy 5

o. Joshua 5

p. Daniel 3

q. Psalm 23

r. 1 Kings 6

s. Daniel 6

t. Ezra 3–6

u. Joshua 10

ANSWERS TO "I FOUND IT! I FOUND IT!"

1. e, 2. g, 3. s, 4. a, 5. 1,n, 6. q, 7. k, 8. d, 9. p, 10. h, 11. b, 12. j, 13. o, 14. f, 15. i, 16. m, 17. c, 18. u, 19. r, 20. t.

....

42

NOW WHERE DID I SEE THAT?

Do you know your New Testament well enough to quickly help a friend locate familiar passages and events in the Bible? Match these. Use your Bible if needed.

PART ONE   BOOK AND CHAPTER

_____ 1. Birth of Jesus—Shepherds   a. Matthew 1, 2

_____ 2. Birth of Jesus—Visit of Magi   b. Matthew 27, 28

_____ 3. Heroes of Faith   c. Mark 15, 16

_____ 4. The Crucifixion and Resurrection   d. Luke 2

_____   (name 4)   e. Luke 15

_____   f. Luke 23, 24

_____   g. John 4

_____ 5. The New Jerusalem   h. John 19, 20

_____ 6. The Seven Churches   i. Acts 2

_____ 7. The Love Chapter   j. 1 Corinthians 13

_____ 8. Parables—Lost Sheep,   k. Hebrews 11

_____   Lost Coin, Lost Son   l. Revelation 2, 3

_____ 9. The Samaritan Woman at the Well   m. Revelation 21

_____10. The Holy Spirit Is Given

Below are either parts of verses or titles to short passages. Match these to their Scripture references.

PART TWO   SCRIPTURE REFERENCE

_____ 1. The Lord's Prayer   a. Matt. 5:3-12

_____ 2. "For God so loved the world . . ."   b. Matt. 6:9-13

_____ 3. "If we confess our sins . . ."   c. Matt. 6:25-34

_____ 4. ". . . when I am weak, then I am   d. Matt. 11:28-30

_____   strong."

_____ 5. The Golden Rule ("Do to others as
            you . . .")   e. Luke 6:31

_____ 6. "Do not let your hearts be troubled . . ."   f. John 3:16

_____ 7. The Beatitudes ("Blessed are . . .")   g. John 10:10

_____ 8. ". . . surrounded by . . . cloud of witnesses . . ."   h. John 14:1-4

_____ 9. Jesus came to bring abundant life.   i. Acts 1:8

_____ 10. ". . . in all things God works for the good . . ."   j. Rom. 6:23

_____ 11. ". . . I stand at the door and knock . . ."   k. Rom. 8:1, 2

_____ 12. ". . . you will receive power . . . the
            Holy Spirit . . ."   l. Rom. 8:28

_____ 13. ". . . there is now no condemnation . . ."   m. 2 Cor. 12:9-10

_____ 14. "Come to me, all . . . weary and burdened . . ."   n. Gal. 6:7-10

_____ 15. "I can do everything through him . . ."   o. Phil. 1:21

_____ 16. ". . . overcame . . . by the blood . . .
            testimony . . ."   p. Phil. 4:13

_____ 17. Sowing, reaping—". . . Let us not become
            weary . . ."   q. Heb. 12:1-3

_____ 18. "For the wages of sin is death, but the gift . . ."   r. 1 John 1:9

_____ 19. "For . . . to live is Christ and to die is gain."   s. Rev. 3:20

_____ 20. ". . . But seek first his kingdom . . ."   t. Rev. 12:11

TURN OVER FOR ANSWERS TO
"NOW WHERE DID I SEE THAT?"

PART TWO:
1. b, 2. f, 3. r, 4. m, 5. e, 6. h, 7. a, 8. q, 9. g, 10. l, 11. s, 12. i, 13. k, 14. d,
15. p, 16. t, 17. n, 18. j, 19. o, 20. c

PART ONE:
1. d, 2. a, 3. k, 4. b, 5. m, 6. f, 7. j, 8. e, 9. g, 10. i

READ ALL ABOUT IT!
Old Testament Headlines

Match *WHAT?* with *WHO?* and *WHERE?* Place the appropriate number from in front of *WHAT?* on the line left of *WHO?* and the proper letter from *WHERE?* at the right of *WHO?*

WHAT?

1. MANKIND'S FIRST SIN
2. ISRAEL'S FIRST KING ANOINTED
3. PROPHET DISAPPEARS IN FRONT OF WITNESS
4. NINETY-YEAR-OLD WOMAN GIVES BIRTH
5. MAGNIFICENT TEMPLE ERECTED
6. FIRST RAINFALL IS DELUGE
7. HEBREW BECOMES RULER IN AFRICAN COUNTRY
8. SACRED LAW GIVEN
9. MADMAN DRIVER
10. MAN KEEPS FAITH THOUGH TORMENTED BY SATAN
11. QUEEN RISKS LIFE FOR THE JEWS
12. KING CYRUS SENDS GROUP TO REBUILD TEMPLE
13. OLDEST LIVING MAN DIES
14. DONKEY TALKS BACK TO MAN
15. WOMAN LEADS ARMY TO VICTORY
16. MOSES ANNOUNCES SUCCESSOR
17. FROM FISH'S BELLY TO NINEVEH
18. FIFTEEN MORE YEARS GRANTED BY GOD
19. A ROYAL MURDER FOR A VINEYARD
20. TWINS BORN

WHERE?

a. Region of Negev
b. Citadel of Susa
c. Over the earth
d. Garden of Eden

e. Beer Lahai Roi
f. From Mount Tabor to Sisera's army
g. Near Jezreel
h. Jerusalem
i. Land close to palace
j. Unknown
k. In king's palace
l. Ramah
m. On the road to Moab
n. Egypt
o. Enroute from Joppa to Tarshish to God's will
p. A distance beyond the Jordan River
q. Mount Sinai
r. Valley near Beth Peor, east of Jordan
s. Uz
t. From Persia to Jerusalem and Judea

WHAT? WHO?

WHO?	WHERE? HELPFUL SCRIPTURE
_____ Joshua	_____ Deut. 4:44-46; 31:1-7
_____ Jehu, the lookout	_____ 2 Kings 9:14-20
_____ Saul, Samuel	_____ 1 Sam. 7:15-17; 8–10:1
_____ Esther, Mordecai, Jews	_____ Esther 1:2; 2-9
_____ Isaac, Rebekah, Esau, Jacob	_____ Gen. 25:11, 21-26
_____ Solomon, David	_____ 2 Chron. 2-7
_____ Balaam and company	_____ Num. 22:9-38
_____ Eve, serpent, Adam	_____ Gen. 3
_____ Ahab, Jezebel, Naboth	_____ 1 Kings 21
_____ Job	_____ Job 1, 2
_____ Jonah	_____ Jonah 1–3
_____ Joseph, Pharaoh	_____ Gen. 41
_____ Elijah, Elisha	_____ 2 Kings 2:7-12
_____ Hezekiah, Isaiah	_____ 2 Kings 20:1-11
_____ Noah, wife, 3 sons, wives	_____ Gen. 6-8
_____ Zerubbabel, Jeshua, Jews	_____ Ezra 1
_____ Deborah, Barak, army, Jael	_____ Judg. 4:4-24
_____ Sarah, Isaac, Abraham	_____ Gen. 17:15-17; 20:1; 21:1-3
_____ God, Moses	_____ Exod. 19–20
_____ Methuselah	_____ Gen. 5:27

....

WHAT?	WHO?	WHERE?
___ 16 ___	Joshua	___ r ___
___ 9 ___	Jehu, the lookout	___ g ___
___ 2 ___	Saul, Samuel	___ l ___
___ 11 ___	Esther, Mordecai, Jews	___ b ___
___ 20 ___	Isaac, Rebekah, Esau, Jacob	___ e ___
___ 5 ___	Solomon, David	___ h ___
___ 14 ___	Balaam and company	___ m ___
___ 1 ___	Eve, serpent, Adam	___ d ___
___ 19 ___	Ahab, Jezebel, Naboth	___ i ___
___ 10 ___	Job	___ s ___
___ 17 ___	Jonah	___ o ___
___ 7 ___	Joseph, Pharaoh	___ n ___
___ 3 ___	Elijah, Elisha	___ p ___
___ 18 ___	Hezekiah, Isaiah	___ k ___
___ 6 ___	Noah, wife, 3 sons, wives	___ c ___
___ 12 ___	Zerubbabel, Jeshua, Jews	___ t ___
___ 15 ___	Deborah, Barak, army, Jael	___ f ___
___ 4 ___	Sarah, Isaac, Abraham	___ a ___
___ 8 ___	God, Moses	___ q ___
___ 13 ___	Methuselah	___ j ___

"READ ALL ABOUT IT."
TURN OVER FOR ANSWERS TO

....

GIVE ME A CLUE

Use this for a Bible study or a quiz. Four clues are given to identify each New Testament book. If quizzing, you earn 4 points for getting the right answer on the first clue, 3 on the second clue, 2 on the third, and 1 on the fourth. With 27 books, 108 points are possible. Write which clue number you were on when writing down your answer. Figure score when completed. Be honest now!

The first clue is a familiar verse from that book. The second one is a fact about the book, the third is the author, the fourth—almost a giveaway.

In testing, rate yourself: 90 to 108 — Outstanding
75 to 89 — Excellent
60 to 74 — Good
0 to 59 — Use this for study

RIDDLE 1. Answer _____ . Gotten on clue # ____ .
1) "Then Peter said, 'I have no silver or gold, but what I have I give you. In the name of Jesus Christ of Nazareth, walk.' "
2) Principal characters include several disciples, Stephen, and Paul.
3) Luke wrote this book.
4) The Holy Spirit comes at Pentecost.

RIDDLE 2. Answer _____ . Gotten on clue # ____ .
1) "Let the word of Christ dwell in you richly as you teach and counsel one another with all wisdom, and as you sing psalms, hymns and spiritual songs with gratitude in your hearts to God."
2) This letter emphasizes Christ as the head of the church.
3) Paul
4) Fill in the blank. Galatians, Ephesians, Philippians, _____ .

RIDDLE 3. Answer _____ . Gotten on clue # ____ .
1) "In a loud voice they sang: 'Worthy is the Lamb, who was slain, to receive power and wealth and wisdom and strength and honor and glory and praise!' "
2) Letters to seven churches appear early in the book.
3) John
4) The prophecy book

RIDDLE 4. Answer _____ . Gotten on clue # ____.
  1) "Therefore, there is now no condemnation for those who are in Christ Jesus."
  2) Contains doctrine and the plan of salvation.
  3) Paul
  4) Written to the people where Paul later was imprisoned

RIDDLE 5. Answer _____ . Gotten on clue # ____.
  1) "Dear friend, do not imitate what is evil but what is good. Anyone who does what is good is from God. Anyone who does what is evil has not seen God."
  2) Written to Gaius
  3) John
  4) The shortest book of the New Testament . . . 15 verses, 299 words

RIDDLE 6. Answer _____ . Gotten on clue # ____.
  1) "For even when we were with you, we gave you this rule: 'If a man will not work, he shall not eat.' "
  2) More about the second coming of Christ
  3) Paul
  4) This book's name is one of the longer ones.

RIDDLE 7. Answer _____ . Gotten on clue # ____.
  1) "Jesus wept."
  2) Much of what Jesus said in the Upper Room is recorded in this book.
  3) "The disciple whom he loved"
  4) This Gospel contains significant material not told by the others.

RIDDLE 8. Answer _____ . Gotten on clue # ____.
  1) "And without faith it is impossible to please God, because anyone who comes to him must believe that he exists and that he rewards those who earnestly seek him."
  2) Written primarily to Hebrew Christians
  3) Uncertain—maybe Paul, Apollos, Barnabas, or someone else
  4) Its chapter 11 is the familiar faith chapter.

RIDDLE 9. Answer _____ . Gotten on clue # ____.
  1) "I press on toward the goal to win the prize for which God has called me heavenward in Christ Jesus."
  2) An epistle written in prison
  3) Paul
  4) It emphasizes joy

RIDDLE 10. Answer _____ . Gotten on clue # ____.
   1) "I appeal to you for my son Onesimus, who became my son while I was in chains."
   2) An appeal to a slave's master
   3) Paul
   4) A book with one chapter

RIDDLE 11. Answer _____ . Gotten on clue # ____.
   1) "Rejoice and be glad, because great is your reward in heaven, for in the same way they persecuted the prophets who were before you."
   2) Contains many references to Jewish prophecies
   3) The disciple who was an ex-tax collector, Levi
   4) The Gospel that was written for the Jews primarily

RIDDLE 12. Answer _____ . Gotten on clue # ____.
   1) "Cast all your anxiety on him because he cares for you."
   2) A book of encouragement and spiritual help
   3) Written by one of the original twelve disciples
   4) Not a Gospel, and his first

RIDDLE 13. Answer _____ . Gotten on clue # ____.
   1) "That is why I am suffering as I am. Yet I am not ashamed, because I know whom I have believed, and am convinced that he is able to guard what I have entrusted to him for that day."
   2) Written from prison to encourage a young man
   3) Paul
   4) The second letter to his "dear son"

RIDDLE 14. Answer _____ . Gotten on clue # ____.
   1) "And Jesus grew in wisdom and stature, and in favor with God and men."
   2) More women are mentioned in this Gospel than the others.
   3) The doctor
   4) Gospel written especially for the Gentiles

RIDDLE 15. Answer _____ . Gotten on clue # ____.
   1) "But someone will say, 'You have faith; I have deeds.' Show me your faith without deeds, and I will show you my faith by what I do."
   2) A practical book on daily living
   3) The brother of Jesus
   4) "Watch your tongue."

RIDDLE 16. Answer _____ . Gotten on clue # ____ .
1) "For the message of the cross is foolishness to those who are perishing, but to us who are being saved it is the power of God."
2) This church is rebuked for its members' immoral practices.
3) Paul
4) Contains the familiar "Love Chapter."

RIDDLE 17. Answer _____ . Gotten on clue # ____ .
1) "I have been crucified with Christ and I no longer live, but Christ lives in me. The life I live in the body, I live by faith in the Son of God, who loved me and gave himself for me."
2) Faith versus law
3) Paul
4) Letter to a church in Asia Minor with six chapters

RIDDLE 18. Answer _____ . Gotten on clue # ____ .
1) "But if we walk in the light, as he is in the light, we have fellowship with one another, and the blood of Jesus, his Son, purifies us from every sin."
2) *Know* and *love* are frequently used words in this book.
3) The disciple whom Jesus loved
4) The first of a trio

RIDDLE 19. Answer _____ . Gotten on clue # ____ .
1) "Snatch others from the fire and save them; to others show mercy, mixed with fear—hating even the clothing stained by corrupted flesh."
2) Warns the church against corrupt teachings
3) Traditionally thought to be Judas, the brother of Jesus.
4) The longest one-chapter book of the New Testament—613 words.

RIDDLE 20. Answer _____ . Gotten on clue # ____ .
1) "Teach the older men to be temperate, worthy of respect, self-controlled, and sound in faith, in love and in endurance."
2) Life-style and character of church leaders listed; what to teach
3) Paul
4) Elders, overseers, bishops are mentioned.

RIDDLE 21. Answer _____ . Gotten on clue # ____ .
1) "But do not forget this one thing, dear friends: With the Lord a day is like a thousand years, and a thousand years are like a day."
2) A call to godliness; corrupt teachers and scoffers will come.

3) Written by one of the original twelve.
4) The second written by this long-ago denier.

RIDDLE 22. Answer _____ . Gotten on clue # ____ .
1) "Don't let anyone look down on you because you are young, but set an example for the believers in speech, in life, in love, in faith and in purity."
2) Recipient of letter had one Jewish and one Gentile parent. His mother is Eunice, his grandmother, Lois.
3) Paul
4) Written to a young man whom Paul considered very dear

RIDDLE 23. Answer _____ . Gotten on clue # ____ .
1) "People were overwhelmed with amazement. 'He has done everything well,' they said. 'He even makes the deaf hear and the mute speak.' "
2) Information gained mainly from Peter
3) Relative of Barnabas, John ____
4) The shortest Gospel

RIDDLE 24. Answer _____ . Gotten on clue # ____ .
1) "For they themselves report what kind of reception you gave us. They tell how you turned to God from idols to serve the living and true God."
2) Message—live pleasing to the Lord in light of the last days.
3) Paul
4) The first written to this church

RIDDLE 25. Answer _____ . Gotten on clue # ____ .
1) "For it is by grace you have been saved, through faith—and this not from yourselves, it is the gift of God."
2) Theme: Christian unity
3) Paul
4) Instructions for wives, husbands, children, parents, slaves, masters. Also: The Armor of God.

RIDDLE 26. Answer _____ . Gotten on clue # ____ .
1) "It has given me great joy to find some of your children living by the truth, just as the Father commanded us."
2) Written to a lady and her children
3) The beloved disciple
4) A short book with 13 verses and 303 words

RIDDLE 27. Answer _____ . Gotten on clue # ____ .

1) "For we are to God the aroma of Christ among those who are being saved and those who are perishing."
2) Tells of personal hardships and the author's perspective
3) Paul
4) The second of two longer epistles

TURN OVER FOR ANSWERS TO
"GIVE ME A CLUE."

1. Acts (3:6)
2. Col. (3:16)
3. Rev. (5:12)
4. Rom. (8:1)
5. 3 John (11)
6. 2 Thess. (3:10)
7. John (11:35)
8. Heb. (11:6)
9. Phil. (3:14)
10. Philem. (10)
11. Matt. (5:12)
12. 1 Pet. (5:7)
13. 2 Tim. (1:12)
14. Luke (2:52)
15. James (2:18)
16. 1 Cor. (1:18)
17. Gal. (2:20)
18. 1 John (1:7)
19. Jude (23)
20. Titus (2:2)
21. 2 Pet. (3:8)
22. 1 Tim. (4:12)
23. Mark (7:37)
24. 1 Thes. (1:9)
25. Eph. (2:8)
26. 2 John (4)
27. 2 Cor. (2:15)

I CAN'T THINK
OF THE RIGHT WORD

This three-part enigma is about some very important Bible words. In Part 1, Bible verses printed are missing one word. After deciding what the omitted word is, go to Part 2 and find the scrambled word that fits in Part 1. Write it on the line, then write the word's letter on the line by the verse. Part 3 has a definition for each word in Part 2. Match those. The verse provides a good contextual clue.

The first one from Part 1 is done for you.

PART 1—BIBLE VERSE.

—f— 1. "The Son is the radiance of God's glory and the exact representation of his being, sustaining all things by his powerful word. After he had provided ___?___ for sins, he sat down at the right hand of the Majesty in heaven." Hebrews 1:3.

_____ 2. "A rebuke impresses a man of ___?___ more than a hundred lashes a fool." Proverbs 17:10.

_____ 3. " '___?___ yourselves and be holy, because I am the LORD your God. Keep my decrees and follow them. I am the LORD, who makes you holy.' " Leviticus 20:7, 8.

_____ 4. "People who want to get rich fall into ___?___ and a trap and into many foolish and harmful desires that plunge men into ruin and destruction." 1 Timothy 6:9.

_____ 5. "Your throne was established long ago; you are from all ___?___ ." Psalm 93:2.

_____ 6. " 'Return, faithless people; I will cure you of ___?___ .' " Jeremiah 3:22a.

_____ 7. "May God himself, the God of peace, ___?___ you through and through. May your whole spirit, soul and body be kept blameless at the coming of our Lord Jesus Christ." 1 Thessalonians 5:23.

_____ 8. "They serve at a ____?____ that is a copy and shadow of what is in heaven. This is why Moses was warned when he was about to build the tabernacle: 'See to it that you make everything according to the pattern shown you on the mountain.' " Hebrews 8:5.

_____ 9. "You will be his ____?____ to all men of what you have seen and heard." Acts 22:15.

_____10. "For you are receiving the goal of your faith, the ____?____ of your souls." 1 Peter 1:9.

_____11. "Because our gospel came to you not simply with words, but also with power, with the Holy Spirit and with deep ____?____ . You know how we lived among you for your sake." 1 Thessalonians 1:5.

_____12. "Godly sorrow brings ____?____ that leads to salvation and leaves no regret, but worldly sorrow brings death." 2 Corinthians 7:10.

_____13. "He was delivered over to death for our sins and was raised to life for our ____?____ ." Romans 4:25.

_____14. "Not only is this so, but we also rejoice in God through our Lord Jesus Christ, through whom we have now received ____?____ ." Romans 5:11.

_____15. " 'Say to the Israelites: "When a man or woman wrongs another in any way and so is unfaithful to the LORD, that person is guilty and must confess the sin he has committed. He must make full ____?____ for his wrong, add one fifth to it and give it all to the person he has wronged.' " Numbers 5:6, 7.

_____16. "In him we have ____?____ through his blood, the forgiveness of sins, in accordance with the riches of God's grace that he lavished on us with all wisdom and understanding." Ephesians 1:7, 8.

_____17. "To be made new in the attitudes of your minds; and to put on the new self, created to be like God in true righteousness and ____?____ ." Ephesians 4:23, 24.

_____18. "Not only so, but we ourselves, who have the firstfruits of the Spirit, groan inwardly as we wait eagerly for our ____?____ as sons, the redemption of our bodies." Romans 8:23.

....

_____19. "In fact, the law requires that nearly everything be cleansed with blood, and without the shedding of blood there is no ____?____ . " Hebrews 9:22.

_____20. "While we wait for the blessed hope—the ____?____ appearing of our great God and Savior, Jesus Christ." Titus 2:13.

_____21. "I want to know Christ and the power of his ____?____ and the fellowship of sharing in his sufferings, becoming like him in his death." Philippians 3:10.

PART 2—UNSCRAMBLE THE SCRAMBLED WORDS and spell correctly at the right.

a. fisycant _____

b. crepeatenn _____

c. pitoodan _____

d. secretcoan _____

e. usogirlo _____

f. fourticinipa _____ purification _____

g. itertney _____

h. relationinocci _____

i. tinsalova _____

j. snefgrosive _____

k. tamepitton _____

l. itonjascifuit _____

m. cutsnaray _____

n. turnsirecore _____

o. siswent _____

p. ostirnuttie _____

q. dentmencirs _____

r. metprideon _____

s. diskingclab _____

t. noccontivi _____

u. shinesol _____

....

PART 3—DEFINITIONS

_____ 1. The process by which sinful men are made acceptable to a holy God.

_____ 2. A holy place set apart for worship of God.

_____ 3. A gift of recognizing or making out clearly something not seen or understood by most.

_____ 4. A spiritual rescue from the consequences of sin; redemption.

_____ 5. A description of God's or God-like beauty, power, or honor.

_____ 6. Infinite or unlimited time—without beginning or end.

_____ 7. The act of God's grace by which sinful man is brought into His redeemed family.

_____ 8. Without sin, partaking of His divine nature.

_____ 9. An invitation or an allurement to sin.

_____10. The process that brings God and man together again.

_____11. Overcoming the power of death by becoming alive again.

_____12. Deliverance paid for by a price—the death of Christ.

__f__ 13. The act of being made clean before God and men.

_____14. God's grace in action—the believer is separated from sin and is dedicated completely to God.

_____15. A sorrow for and a turning from sin to God.

_____16. God's pardoning of our sins.

_____17. The setting apart, or dedicating of something or someone for God's use.

_____18. To revert to sin or wrongdoing.

_____19. The act of giving back to an owner what has been taken wrongfully.

_____20. The process of feeling condemnation for sin by the Holy Spirit.

_____21. Experiencing something enough to be able to tell about it with authority.

PART 1	PART 2	PART 3
1. f	a. sanctify	1. l
2. q	b. repentance	2. m
3. d	c. adoption	3. q
4. k	d. consecrate	4. i
5. g	e. glorious	5. e
6. s	f. purification	6. g
7. a	g. eternity	7. c
8. m	h. reconciliation	8. u
9. o	i. salvation	9. k
10. i	j. forgiveness	10. h
11. t	k. temptation	11. n
12. b	l. justification	12. r
13. l	m. sanctuary	13. f
14. h	n. resurrection	14. a
15. p	o. witness	15. b
16. r	p. restitution	16. j
17. u	q. discernment	17. d
18. c	r. redemption	18. s
19. j	s. backsliding	19. p
20. e	t. conviction	20. t
21. n	u. holiness	21. o

TURN OVER FOR ANSWERS TO
"I CAN'T THINK OF THE RIGHT WORD."

IT'S VERY COMMON

Three out of the four in each group below have something in common in Bible content. *Strike out the odd one*. Write what the other three have in common on the line. Helpful scriptures are listed beneath the exercise.

1. The Lost Coin, The Mustard Seed, _____
   The Persistent Widow, Feeding the Five Thousand

2. Bethany, Jerusalem, Judea, Bethlehem _____

3. James, Paul, Peter, John _____

4. Lydia, Priscilla, Phoebe, Rebekah _____

5. 1 Timothy, Titus, Romans, James _____

6. Colossians, Jude, Philemon, 2 John _____

7. John, Paul, Luke, Mark _____

8. James, Stephen, John, John the Baptist _____

9. Peter's mother-in-law, Lazarus, _____
   Jairus' daughter, the son of the widow of Nain

10. Savior, Messiah, Son of God, Evangelist _____

11. Joanna, Sapphira, Susanna, _____
    Mary Magdalene

12. Andrew, Thomas, Aquila, Matthew _____

13. Abraham, Moses, David, Caleb _____

14. "Blessed are the peacemakers . . ." _____
    "Blessed are you when people insult you . . ."
    "Blessed is the man who does not walk in the counsel of the wicked . . ."
    "Blessed are the pure in heart . . ."

15. Thomas, Silas, Barnabas, John Mark _____

16. Has the most memorized verse _____
    Has the Sermon on the Mount

Has the Upper Room Discourse given by Jesus

17. Bethlehem, Nazareth, Capernaum, Egypt _____

18. Solomon, Eli, Jonah, Samuel _____

19. Ephesians, Philippians, Colossians,
    1 Corinthians _____

20. John, Mary Magdalene, Nicodemus,
    Joseph of Arimathea _____

HELPFUL SCRIPTURES: (1) Luke 9:10-17; 13:18, 19; 15:8-10; 18:1-8. (2) Map of Palestine in Jesus' times (back of many Bibles). (3) Matt. 10:2-4; Acts 13:9. (4) Gen. 24:29; Acts 16:14; 18:2; Rom. 16:1. (5) Rom. 1:1; 1 Tim. 1:1; Titus 1:1; James 1:1. (6) Look at each book. (7) Consider books. (8) Matt. 14:6-12; Acts 7:54-60; 12:1, 2. (9) Matt. 8:14, 15; Mark 5:21-43; Luke 7:11-15; John 11:1-44. (10) Luke 1:35; 2:11; John 1:41. (11) Luke 8:2, 3; Acts 5:1, 5-10. (12) Matt. 10:2-4; Acts 18:2-4. (13) Heb. 11:17, 24, 32. (14) Ps. 1:1; Matt. 5:3-11. (15) Acts 1:13; 15:37-40. (16) Matt. 5–7; John 3:16; 11:35; 13-17. (17) Matt. 2:1, 14, 21-23; 4:12-13. (18) Matt. 6:29; 12:40; Heb. 11:32. (19) See order of books. (20) Matt. 27:57-61; John 19:38-40

ANSWERS TO "IT'S VERY COMMON."

Strike out:	The rest have in common:
1. The Five Thousand (a real happening)	Parables told by Jesus
2. Judea (a country)	Cities or towns
3. Paul (came later)	Part of Jesus' 12 disciples
4. Rebekah (Old Testament times)	Lived in New Testament times
5. James (written by James)	Paul's letters or epistles
6. Colossians (has 4 chapters)	Books with only one chapter
7. Paul (wrote letters or epistles)	Gospel writers
8. John (death not mentioned)	Martyrs mentioned in Scripture
9. Peter's mother-in-law (sick—healed)	Raised from the dead by Jesus
10. Evangelist	Names given to Jesus
11. Sapphira (lied and died)	True followers of Jesus
12. Aquila	Part of Jesus' 12 disciples
13. Caleb (not mentioned in New Testament)	Mentioned in New Testament
14. "Blessed is the man . . ." (Ps. 1:1)	Beatitudes found in Matthew
15. Thomas (not mentioned with Paul)	Traveled with Paul at some time
16. Second one (found in Matthew)	Found in the Gospel of John
17. Capernaum (moved there as adult)	Places Jesus lived in childhood
or Egypt (country where Jesus lived)	*or* Towns where Jesus lived
18. Eli (not mentioned in New Testament)	Mentioned in the New Testament
19. 1 Corinthians (out of order in Bible)	Are in order in the Bible
20. John (not mentioned as being there)	At the burial of Jesus

....

62

CHRISTMAS IS MY FAVORITE HOLIDAY

Some concepts about the Christmas story are not exactly biblical.

How well do you know the Bible's account of the Christmas story? Find out by taking this as a test. You may be surprised. Use *T* for true facts straight from the Bible. Label *F* for false and *U* for unclear or not said precisely so in the Scripture.

_____ 1. Five woman are listed in the genealogies of Jesus in Matthew 1 and Luke 3:23-37.

_____ 2. The genealogies in Matthew and Luke are identical, except Matthew starts with Abraham and goes to Joseph; while Luke takes the reverse route and goes back to Adam. (See above scriptures.)

_____ 3. The angel Gabriel appeared to Mary, telling her she would give birth to the Son of God. (Luke 1:26-33)

_____ 4. After her pregnancy began, Mary traveled to visit awhile with her relative Elizabeth. (Luke 1:36, 39)

_____ 5. Mary and Joseph's hometown was Jerusalem. (Luke 1:26; 2:4)

_____ 6. The name *Jesus* means one who can save us from our sins. (Matt. 1:21)

_____ 7. *Immanuel* means "God with us." (Matt. 1:23)

_____ 8. Joseph never questioned Mary's virginity when he learned of her condition. (Matt. 1:19-24)

_____ 9. Mary and Joseph went to Bethlehem on government business. (Luke 2:1, 2)

_____10. The innkeeper had no room for them in an inn, so he provided them a place to stay with the animals. (Luke 2:7)

_____ 11. Jesus was born in a barn or stable. (Luke 2:7)

_____ 12. One angel announced Jesus' birth to the shepherds in the fields before the rest of the angels appeared. (Luke 2:8-13)

_____ 13. The angels sang in heavenly chorus, "Glory to God in the highest, and on earth peace to men on whom his favor rests." (Luke 2:13, 14)

_____ 14. The number of shepherds who visited Jesus is unknown. (Luke 2:15, 16)

_____ 15. A star led Magi from the east in search of the Christ child. (Matt. 2:2)

_____ 16. Herod knew his Scriptures well enough to tell the wise men to go to Bethlehem. (Matt. 2: 3, 4)

_____ 17. Three Magi had made this trip to see the Babe. (Matt. 2:1, 2, 7, 9-12)

_____ 18. The star was spotted again by the wise men after they left Herod. (Matt. 2:9-10)

_____ 19. The wise men found Jesus lying in a manger. (Matt. 2:11)

_____ 20. The Magi gave gifts of gold, incense (frankincense), and myrrh. (Matt. 2:11)

_____ 21. The wise men were warned in a dream not to return to Herod. (Matt. 2:12)

_____ 22. The angel of the Lord told Joseph to take Mary and the Baby and escape to Egypt. (Matt. 2:13)

_____ 23. Feeling threatened by the possible birth of a Jewish king, Herod ordered that all boys, two years old and younger, be killed. (Matt. 2:16)

_____ 24. After Herod's death Joseph, Mary and Jesus returned to Bethlehem. (Matt. 2:21-23)

_____ 25. On their way back from Egypt, Mary and Joseph took Jesus to the Temple for circumcision and presentation to the Lord. Simeon and Anna recognized him as the Messiah then. (Luke 2:21)

....

True: 1, 3, 4, 6, 7, 9, 12, 14, 15, 18, 20, 21, 22, 23

1. T.
   They are all found in Matthew. Tamar, v. 3; Rahab, v. 5; Ruth, v. 5; mother of Solomon, "Solomon, whose mother had been Uriah's wife" v. 6; Mary, "Joseph, the husband of Mary" v. 16.
2. F.
   "From Abraham to David, the genealogies of Matthew and Luke are almost the same, but from David on they are different. . . . Likely . . . Matthew follows the line of Joseph (Jesus' legal father), while Luke emphasizes that of Mary (Jesus' blood relative). Although tracing a genealogy through the mother's side was unusual, so was the virgin birth. Luke's explanation here that Jesus was the son of Joseph, 'so it was thought' (v. 23), brings to mind his explicit virgin birth statement (1:34, 35) and suggests the importance of the role of Mary in Jesus' genealogy." From *The NIV Study Bible*, Kenneth Barker, gen. ed. (Grand Rapids: Zondervan, 1985), p. 1543.
5. F.
   Nazareth
8. F.
   Joseph considered divorce, but an angel revealed the real truth.
10. U.
   The Bible doesn't say so, though he may have.
11. U.
   No mention of barn, stable, or animals is made. Mary "wrapped Him in clothes and placed him in a manger," a perfect baby bed anywhere.
13. F.
   They appeared, "praising God and *saying*".
16. F.
   He had to ask the chief priests and teachers of the Law.
17. U or F.
   There was more than one wise man, because pronoun "we" is used in conversation. Three kinds of gifts could have been brought by 2 or 22.
19. U or F.
   They found the Baby in a house. A manger is doubtful.
24. F.
   They returned to Nazareth.
25. F.
   They went to the Temple when Jesus was 8 days old.

TURN OVER FOR ANSWERS TO
"CHRISTMAS IS MY FAVORITE HOLIDAY".

....

BUILDING CHARACTER

The list below describes or characterizes a true Christian according to Scripture. Fill in the missing letters. Then find them in the word search puzzle. Helpful scriptures: Acts 1:8; Rom. 5:3, 4; 2 Cor. 6:6; Gal. 5:22, 23; Eph. 5:9; James 3:17, 18; 2 Pet. 1:5-7.

LIST:

c __ __ s __ __ e __ a __ __   c __ __ r __ c __ __ __

f __ __ __ __ f __ __ n __ __ __   g e __ __ __ __ n __ __ __

g __ __ i __ __   g __ __ __ i __ __ s__

g __ __ __ __ e __ __   g __ o __ __ __ g

h __ __ __   i __ p __ __ __ i __ l

j __ __   k __ __ __ __ e __ s

k __ __ __ l __ __ __ __   l __ __ __

m __ __ c __ __ __ l   p a__ __ __ __ c __

p __ __ __ e   p __ __ c __ __ a __ __ r

p __ __ s __ v __ __ __ n __ __   p __ __ i __ __

r __ __ __ t __ __ __ s __ __ __ s   s __ __ __ c __ __ t __ __ __

s __ __ c __ __ __   s __ __ __ i __ __ i __ e

t __ __ __ h   u __ __ e__ s __ __ __ __ __ __ g

                    w__ __ n __ __ __ e __

```
M  C  H  A  R  A  C  T  E  R  G  I  V  E  M
E  O  E  C  N  A  R  E  V  E  S  R  E  P  G
R  G  O  O  D  N  E  S  S  U  R  A  E  S  N
C  O  I  N  I  S  G  U  Y  N  R  A  D  S  I
I  D  V  S  M  S  P  O  R  D  C  P  S  E  V
F  L  I  I  P  E  J  G  S  E  S  E  U  L  I
U  I  N  D  A  N  S  N  A  R  N  A  B  F  G
L  N  S  E  R  L  S  I  P  S  S  C  M  C  P
E  E  S  R  T  U  E  W  U  T  E  E  I  O  R
C  S  S  A  I  F  N  O  R  A  S  M  S  N  A
N  S  E  T  A  H  E  R  I  N  S  A  S  T  I
E  L  N  E  L  T  L  G  T  D  E  K  I  R  S
I  O  D  I  H  I  T  G  Y  I  N  E  V  O  E
T  V  N  G  O  A  N  R  S  N  T  R  E  L  T
A  E  I  O  P  F  E  M  X  G  I  V  I  G  H
P  R  K  L  E  E  G  D  E  L  W  O  N  K  E
S  I  N  C  E  R  E  H  T  U  R  T  G  I  L
```

ANSWERS TO "BUILDING CHARACTER":

```
M C H A R A C T E R   G I V E   M
E O E C N A R E V E S R E P     G
R O G O O D N E S S U R A E   S N
C D I N S   I M S G U Y   N R A D S I
I I V I S   S P O Y   D C P S L V
F L I D P J G S R E E U L I
U I N E S S N I A R S A B F G
L N S R A S N E P S C M C P
E E A T E N W U S E M O R
C S S A F O R A S M S N A
N S E T I H L R I N A S T I
E S N I A L G Y D K I R S
I L D O H I T E R V E O E
T O I G P O A F E M X G I V L T
A V E O H L N I R G I H H
P R K L E   G D E L W O N K   E
S I N C E R E   H T U R T G I L
```

List

considerate	love
character	merciful
faithfulness	patience
gentleness	peace
giving	peacemaker
godliness	perseverance
goodness	purity
growing	righteousness
hope	self-control
impartial	sincere
joy	submissive
kindness	truth
knowledge	understanding
	witnesses

68

HEAVEN—THE NEW JERUSALEM (WHAT'S IT LIKE?)

The Book of Revelation gives us a glimpse of what heaven will be like. Mere words were inadequate to describe what John saw, but he related it to things as they appear on earth. However, heaven is much more glorious and beautiful than we are capable of visualizing here on earth.

To break the code of descriptions, move one letter up in the alphabet—an *a* is really a *b*, a *b* is a *c*, and so on through the alphabet. Finally, *z* is an *a*.

1. MN RDZ. (21:1)

2. CVDKKHMF NE FNC VHSG LDM. (21:3)

3. MN LNQD SDZQR. (21:4)

4. MN LNQD CDZSG. (21:4)

5. MN LNQD OZHM. (21:4)

6. NUDQBNLDQR HMGDQHS ZKK NE SGHR. (21:7)

7. RGHMDR VHSG SGD FKNQX NE FNC. (21:11)

8. AQHKKHZMS KHJD Z UDQX OQDBHNTR IDVDK—IZRODQ, BKDZQ ZR BQXRSZK. (21:11)

9. SGD VZKK HR LZCD NE IZRODQ, SGD BHSX NE OTQD FNKC. (21:18)

10. CDBNQZSDC VHSG DUDQX JHMC NE OQDBHNTR RSNMD. (21:19)

11. SVDKUD FZSDR—DZBG LZCD NE Z RHMFKD ODZQK. (21:21)

12. SGD KNQC FNC ZKLHFGSX ZMC SGD KZLA ZQD SGD SDLOKD. (21:22)

13. SGD FKNQX NE FOC FHUDR HS KHFGS, ZMC SGD KZLA HR HSR KZLO. (21:23)

14. MN MHFGS SGDQD. (21:25)

15. MNSGHMF HLOTQD VHKK DUDQ DMSDQ HS. (21:27)

16. NMKX SGNRD VGNRD MZLDR ZQD VQHSSDM HM SGD KZLA'R ANNJ NE KHED VHKK DMSDQ. (21:27)

17. Z QHUDQ EKNVR EQNL SGD SGQNMD NE FNC ZMC NE SGD KZLA. (22:1)

18. SQDD NE KHED SGDQD XHDKCR HSR EQTHS DUDQX LNMSG. (22:2)

19. MN LNQD SGHQRS NQ GTMFDQ. (7:16)

20. VNMCDQETK RHMFHMF ZMC LTRHB. (14:2, 3; 15:2, 3)

TURN OVER FOR ANSWERS TO
"HEAVEN—THE NEW JERUSALEM."

20. WONDERFUL SINGING AND MUSIC.
19. NO MORE THIRST OR HUNGER.
18. TREE OF LIFE THERE YIELDS ITS FRUIT EVERY MONTH.
17. A RIVER FLOWS FROM THE THRONE OF GOD AND OF THE LAMB.
16. ONLY THOSE WHOSE NAMES ARE WRITTEN IN THE LAMB'S BOOK OF LIFE WILL ENTER.
15. NOTHING IMPURE WILL EVER ENTER IT.
14. NO NIGHT THERE.
13. THE GLORY OF GOD GIVES IT LIGHT, AND THE LAMB IS ITS LAMP.
12. THE LORD GOD ALMIGHTY AND THE LAMB ARE THE TEMPLE.
11. TWELVE GATES—EACH MADE OF A SINGLE PEARL.
10. DECORATED WITH EVERY KIND OF PRECIOUS STONE.
9. THE WALL IS MADE OF JASPER, THE CITY OF PURE GOLD.
8. BRILLIANT LIKE A VERY PRECIOUS JEWEL—JASPER, CLEAR AS CRYSTAL.
7. SHINES WITH THE GLORY OF GOD.
6. OVERCOMERS INHERIT ALL OF THIS.
5. NO MORE PAIN.
4. NO MORE DEATH.
3. NO MORE TEARS.
2. DWELLING OF GOD WITH MEN.
1. NO SEA.

MAKE ME WISE, O LORD

When the puzzle below is completed, you will be able to read Proverbs 2:6. To make words, fit the proper letters from each column into the boxes directly above them. Of course, the letters are out of order. Use each letter only once. Dark squares are the spaces between words. The first letter is filled in for you.

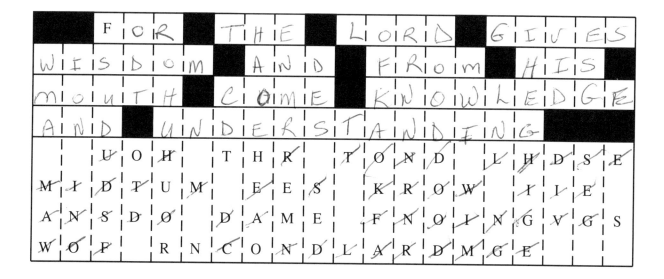

ANSWER TO "MAKE ME WISE, O LORD"

Proverbs 2:6—"For the LORD gives wisdom, and from His mouth come knowledge and understanding."

JESUS, THE GREAT I AM

Wow! The strangest thing has happened. All consonants have disappeared from the "I AM" list below. Could you please help me by writing in the missing consonants? All of these quotations are from the book of John (NIV), except the last six, which come from his last book.

1. I a__ __ __e __ __e a__ o__ __i __ e. (6:35)

2. I a__ __ __o__ a __ o __ e. (8:23)

3. . . . __e __ o __ e A__ __a __a __ __a__ __o __ __ , I a __. (8:58)

4. I a__ __ __e __i __ __ __ o __ __ __e __o __ __ __ __. (9:5)

5. I a__ __ __e __a __ e. (10:9)

6. I a__ __ __e __o o __ __ __e __ __ e __ __. (10:14)

7. I a__ __o __'__ __on . (10:36)

8. I a__ __ __e __e __u __ __e __ __i o __ a __ __ __ __e __i __ e . (11:25)

9. Y__ __ __a __ __ __e "__e a __ __e __" a __ __ __o __ __ , a __ __ __i __ __ __ __ __ __o, __o__ __ __a __ i __ __ __a __ I a __. (13:13)

10. I a__ __ __e __a __ a __ __ __ __e __ __u __ __ a __ __ __ __e __i __ e. (14:6)

11. I a__ __ __e __ __u e __i __ e. (15:1)

12. I a__ __ __e A__ __ __a a__ __ __ __e O __e __a. (__ e __ e __ a __i o __ 1:8)

13. I a__ __ __e __i __ __ __ a __ __ __ __e __a __ __ . (__ e __ e __a __ i o __ 1:17)

14. I a__ __ __e __i__i__ __ O__e. (__e__e__a__io__ 1:18)

15. I a__ __e __ __o __ea__ __ __e__ __ea__ __ __ a__ __
    __i__ __ __. (__e__e__a__io__ 2:23)

16. I a__ __o__i__ __ __oo__. (__e__e__a__io__ 3:11)

17. I a__ __ __e __oo__ a__ __ __ __e o__ __ __ __ __ __i__ __
    o__ __a__i__, a__ __ __ __e __ __i__ __ __ __ __o__ __i__ __
    __ __a__ (__e__e__a__io__ 22:16)

TURN OVER FOR ANSWERS TO
"JESUS, THE GREAT I AM."

(all quotations)

1. I am the bread of life.
2. I am from above.
3. . . . before Abraham was born, I am.
4. I am the light of the world.
5. I am the gate.
6. I am the good shepherd.
7. I am God's Son.
8. I am the resurrection and the life.
9. You call me "Teacher" and "Lord," and rightly so, for that is what I am.
10. I am the way and the truth and the life.
11. I am the true vine.
12. I am the Alpha and Omega.
13. I am the First and the Last.
14. I am the Living One.
15. I am he who searches hearts and minds.
16. I am coming soon.
17. I am the Root and the Offspring of David, and the bright Morning Star.

GOD'S INVITATION TO CALL

Below are groups of numbers that when decoded will form a Bible verse. From the telephone, choose a letter to correspond to the number in the puzzle. To help you, a few correct letters are in place. Remember, a *2* might mean an *a*, *b*, or *c*. A pencil with an eraser is helpful in doing this verse.

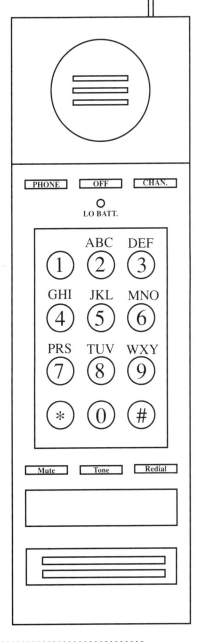

C   w
2255   86   63   263   4   9455

       n   o
    267937   968   263   8355   968

         e   c
    47328   263   867327242253

  h   n
844647   968   36   668   5669.

           J   i
        53736424   33:3

PHONE   OFF   CHAN.

LO BATT.

ABC   DEF
1   2   3

GHI   JKL   MNO
4   5   6

PRS   TUV   WXY
7   8   9

*   0   #

Mute   Tone   Redial

ANSWER TO "GOD'S INVITATION TO CALL":

Call to me and I will answer you and tell you great and unsearchable things you do not know. (Jeremiah 33:3)

GOD'S PROMISE TO THOSE WHO CALL

Below are numbers representing words of a Bible verse. From the telephone, choose a letter to correspond to the number in the puzzle. To help you, a few correct letters are in place. Remember, a *2* might mean an *a*, *b*, or *c*, etc.

367,   "38379663   946   22557
           E   h   l

(E)
367,   "38379663   946   22557
       "E   h   l

66   843   6263   63   843
            n

r
5673   9455   23   72833."
                    a

o
766267   10:13

ANSWER TO "GOD'S PROMISE TO THOSE WHO CALL":

for, "Everyone who calls on the name of the Lord will be saved." (Romans 10:13)

A LOVE MESSAGE FROM GOD

This heart contains one of the many love messages found in God's Word. Start where the arrow points—*H*. After writing that letter on the line below, count around to the right and add every fourth letter to your message. (*O* is the second letter, *W* the third, and so on.) After *every* letter on the outer row is used, drop down to the next one. Continue in the same way, doing each row completely before passing on to the next one. Use every letter, punctuation mark and number. The Bible reference ends the message.

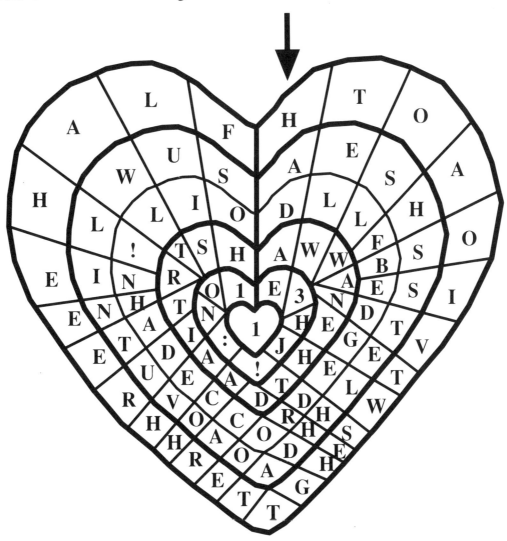

ANSWER FOR "A LOVE MESSAGE FROM GOD":

"How great is the love the Father has lavished on us, that we should be called children of God! And that is what we are!" (1 John 3:1*a*)

A HEALTHY HEART

"The LORD searches every heart."—1 Chron. 28:9c

"God knows your hearts."—Luke 16:15b

How healthy is your heart? The Bible gives several descriptions of the heart—positive and negative. Here is a list of healthy qualities for you to find in your Bible.

PROCEDURE: 1. Find and read each reference through. 2. Then write down each appropriate heart description.

BEGINNING TIME (on the clock): _____

1. A _____ ♥. 1 Tim. 1:5

2. A _____ and _____ ♥. Ps. 51:17

3. An _____ ♥. Ezek. 11:19

4. ♥ was _____ _____ . 2 Chron. 15:17

5. _____ of ♥. Col. 3:22

6. ♥ at _____ . Prov. 14:30

7. _____ and _____ in ♥. Matt. 11:29

8. ♥ is _____ . Ps. 108:1

9. _____ of ♥. Jer. 32:39

10. ♥ s _____ within us. Luke 24:32

11. ♥ will _____ . Isa. 66:14

12. Do not _____ _____ ♥s _____ _____ .
    John 14:27

13. _____ my ♥_____ Ps. 119:32

14. _____ ♥. Ezek. 18:31

15. _____ your ♥s. 2 Thess. 2:17

16. _____ ♥. Prov. 15:15

17. _____ in your ♥s. Col. 3:16

18. _____ it (the law) with _____ _____ ♥.
    Ps. 119:34

19. have _____ the ♥s. Philem. 7

20. _____ and _____ ♥. Luke 8:15

21. _____ ♥. Eccles. 8:5

22. He _____ your ♥s. 1 Thess. 3:13

ENDING TIME: _____

TIME TAKEN: _____ minutes

TURN OVER FOR ANSWERS TO
"A HEALTHY HEART."

NOW go back and reread the statements. IS YOUR HEART HEALTHY?

GREAT! 10 minutes—CONGRATULATIONS, you're faster than I am.

If you are 100% correct and completed this in 15 minutes—GOOD! 12 minutes—

1. pure, 2. broken, contrite, 3. undivided, 4. fully committed, 5. sincerity, 6. peace, 7. gentle and humble, 8. steadfast, 9. singleness, 10. burning, 11. rejoice, 12. let your . . . be troubled, 13. set . . . free, 14. new, 15. encourage, 16. cheerful, 17. gratitude, 18. obey . . . all my, 19. refreshed, 20. noble . . . good, 21. wise, 22. strengthen.

READ ALL ABOUT IT!
New Testament Headlines

Match *WHAT?* with *WHO?* and *WHERE?* Place the appropriate number from in front of *WHAT?* on the line left of *WHO?* and the proper letter from *WHERE?* at the right of *WHO?*

WHAT?

1. JESUS INCLUDES BEATITUDES IN SERMON
2. MESSIAH CARES ABOUT SAMARITANS TOO
3. PASSENGERS AND CREW SURVIVE SHIPWRECK
4. PHARISEE GETS LESSON ON BEING BORN AGAIN
5. DEAD SON MIRACULOUSLY LIVES
6. ASCENDED INTO HEAVEN
7. END TIMES REVEALED TO ELDERLY DISCIPLE
8. PHARISEE PERSECUTOR CONVERTED
9. SANITY RESTORED AFTER LEGIONS OF DEMONS CAST OUT
10. NO FUNDS AVAILABLE, BUT HEALING IS
11. JESUS SERVED BY FRIENDS IN THEIR HOME
12. RESURRECTION FOLLOWS EARTHQUAKE
13. TREE CLIMBER SEES ERROR OF HIS WAY
14. WINE MADE FROM WATER?
15. A SPECTACULAR BIRTH ANNOUNCEMENT
16. TEMPTER ATTEMPTS TEMPTING THE SON OF GOD
17. EARTHQUAKE CONVERSION
18. CHRISTIANITY—HOLY SPIRIT IS FOR GENTILES TOO
19. THREE EXECUTED ON CROSSES
20. LENGTHY PREACHING RESULTS IN DEATH

WHERE?

a. cemetery

b. Troas

c. beautiful (temple gate)

d. vicinity of Bethany

e. somewhere in Jerusalem

f. near island of Malta

g. on road to, and in, Damascus

h. Sychar, Jacob's well

i. Nain

j. Golgotha

k. in a Bethany home

l. fields near Bethlehem

m. Jericho

n. Caesarea

o. desert

p. Cana in Galilee

q. region of Gerasenes

r. mountainside

s. Philippi

t. Isle of Patmos

WHAT? WHO?

_____ Jesus, widow, and son

_____ Peter, John, a crippled man

_____ A woman, Jesus

_____ Mary, Jesus, wedding party

_____ Nicodemus, Jesus

_____ Mary, Martha, Jesus

_____ Zacchaeus, Jesus

_____ Jesus, devil

WHERE? HELPFUL SCRIPTURE

_____ Luke 7:11-16

_____ Acts 3:1-10

_____ John 4:5-42

_____ John 2:1-11

_____ John 2:23–3:21

_____ Luke 10:38-42; John 11:1

_____ Luke 19:1-10

_____ Luke 4:1-13

WHAT? WHO?	WHERE? HELPFUL SCRIPTURE
____ Man living in cemetery, Jesus	____ Mark 5:1-20
____ Jesus, disciples, crowd	____ Matt. 5–7
____ Peter, Cornelius	____ Acts 10
____ Saul, others, Jesus, Ananias	____ Acts 9:3-19
____ Paul, Silas, Philippian jailer	____ Acts 16:12, 16-34
____ Paul, people, Eutychus	____ Acts 20:6-12
____ Jesus, two robbers	____ Mark 15:22-37
____ Jesus, disciples, two angels	____ Luke 24:50-51; Acts 1:6-11
____ Paul, sailors	____ Acts 27–28:1
____ women, angel, guards, Jesus	____ Matthew 28:1-10
____ John, Jesus Christ	____ Book of Revelation
____ Jesus, angels, shepherds	____ Luke 2:8-14

ANSWERS TO "READ ALL ABOUT IT"

WHAT?	WHO?	WHERE?
__ 5 __	Jesus, widow, and son	__ i __
__ 10 __	Peter, John, a crippled man	__ c __
__ 2 __	A woman, Jesus	__ h __
__ 14 __	Mary, Jesus, wedding party	__ p __
__ 4 __	Nicodemus, Jesus	__ e __
__ 11 __	Mary, Martha, Jesus	__ k __
__ 13 __	Zacchaeus, Jesus	__ m __
__ 16 __	Jesus, devil	__ o __
__ 9 __	Man living in cemetery, Jesus	__ q __
__ 1 __	Jesus, disciples, crowd	__ r __
__ 18 __	Peter, Cornelius	__ n __
__ 8 __	Saul, others, Jesus, Ananias	__ g __
__ 17 __	Paul, Silas, Philippian jailer	__ s __
__ 20 __	Paul, people, Eutychus	__ b __
__ 19 __	Jesus, two robbers	__ j __
__ 6 __	Jesus, disciples, two angels	__ d __
__ 3 __	Paul, sailors	__ f __
__ 12 __	women, angel, guards, Jesus	__ a __
__ 7 __	John, Jesus Christ	__ t __
__ 15 __	Jesus, angels, shepherds	__ l __